CW01512566

Original title:

Carmine Fog Beneath the Phoenix Jut

Copyright © 2025 Swan Charm

All rights reserved.

Author: Eliora Lumiste

ISBN HARDBACK: 978-1-80563-505-5

ISBN PAPERBACK: 978-1-80565-026-3

Silhouettes of Flame in Hidden Valleys

In valleys deep where shadows creep,
The silhouettes of flame do leap.
With whispers soft, they dance and sway,
Beneath the moon's enchanting ray.

A flicker bright through tangled trees,
An ember's warmth in evening's breeze.
The secrets guard by silent shades,
As night descends, the light cascades.

Through misty dreams, the spirits tread,
In colors bold, from passion spread.
Each glowing spark, a tale retold,
Of love and loss and hearts so bold.

In hidden realms where legends weave,
The brave will find what they believe.
A path unwound, a quest begun,
In the embrace of flame and sun.

As dawn unfolds on whispered wings,
The valleys sing of ancient things.
Yet still they hush, these flames entwined,
Their flickering hearts in shadows bind.

Whispering Red Across Forgotten Trails

Through the woods where shadows play,
Whispers linger, lost in sway.
Crimson leaves on paths untold,
Secrets woven, stories bold.

Echoes of a time long gone,
In rustling branches, a silent song.
Footprints hidden in the dust,
Speak of journeys, dreams and trust.

Each bend reveals a tale anew,
Of laughter shared and skies so blue.
With every step, the past will sigh,
A tapestry where memories lie.

Embered Echoes of a Celestial Day

The sun dips low, a fiery flare,
Painting skies with warmth and care.
Embers dance in twilight's glow,
Sparking dreams that softly flow.

Stars awaken, bright and bold,
Whispers of the night unfold.
In the calm, they twinkle bright,
Guardians of the tender night.

Celestial songs weave through the air,
Ethereal tales, secrets to share.
With every breath, the cosmos sighs,
As hope ignites in velvet skies.

Flare of Ancient Spirits in the Fade

In the dawn where shadows creep,
Ancient spirits wake from sleep.
Flickers of light in the dusky haze,
Elders dance in forgotten ways.

Their laughter rings through time and space,
Echoes of a long-lost grace.
With every flicker, a memory flows,
Bringing warmth as the soft wind blows.

In the fade, their stories blend,
A tapestry that will not end.
With flares of light, they guide the night,
In whispers soft, their spirits bright.

Crimson Breath in the Misty Air

Morning breaks with a gentle sigh,
Misty veils where shadows lie.
Crimson light, a fleeting breath,
Awakening life from dreams of death.

The world stirs with quiet grace,
Nature paints in this sacred space.
Each moment glows, a soft caress,
In the air, a whispered bless.

As dawn unfolds with vibrant hue,
Promises of the day anew.
With every heartbeat, life unbends,
In the mist, the magic blends.

Ruby Shroud on the Horizon's Edge

On the cusp of twilight's grace,
Ruby whispers weave and trace,
The sun dips low, in blushing hue,
While shadows play, a dance anew.

Waves of warmth kiss the cool air,
On the edge, one can't help but stare,
The horizon glows, a molten thread,
Through the calm, the promise spread.

Voices echo in the still night,
A tapestry of love and light,
In the depths, a secret's kept,
Where dreams and hopes are gently swept.

Beneath the shroud, mysteries unfold,
Tales of courage, bold and untold,
A world awaits beyond retreat,
Where heart and spirit whisper sweet.

With every heartbeat, skies ignite,
The promise of a brand new light,
For in this hour, all things align,
A ruby shroud, a path divine.

Scarlet Veil of the Rebirth

In the quiet dawn, a veil unfurls,
Scarlet whispers dance and twirl,
Beneath the moon's soft fading glow,
The spirit stirs, begins to grow.

From ashes sprouts a vibrant bloom,
A song of life dispels the gloom,
Each petal soaked in tender light,
A promise found in day's new sight.

Through tangled woods and woven dreams,
Reality is never as it seems,
With every dawn, rebirth defined,
A tapestry of love entwined.

Scarlet threads in fate's design,
Woven through the fabric divine,
A journey beckons with each breath,
Through life, through loss, through love, through death.

So let the heart in wonder soar,
Beyond the veil, to distant shore,
For every end is but a start,
In the scarlet veil, find your heart.

The Glow of Fire-Kissed Dreams

By the flicker of a fireside,
Whispers of dreams begin to glide,
In the embers, stories burn bright,
Illuminating the quiet night.

Each flame a wish, a hope in flight,
Dancing shadows, pure delight,
With every spark, aspirations rise,
In this glow, truth never lies.

Echoes of laughter fill the air,
Close your eyes, let go of despair,
In the warmth, the heart finds peace,
In the glow, our fears release.

Casting spells in the midnight blue,
Fire-kissed dreams, they soon pursue,
Through the wild, enchantment streams,
Carried softly on starlit beams.

As dawn awakens, cherish this night,
For in the dark, we find the light,
In every dream where courage gleams,
Is the glow of our fire-kissed dreams.

Beneath a Shroud of Sanguine Skies

As the sun dips, colors bleed,
Underneath, a world takes heed,
Sanguine skies, a haunting sight,
Where shadows merge with fading light.

The whispers of the wind grow loud,
A gentle hymn beneath each cloud,
With every heartbeat, time suspends,
In this realm, where all transcends.

Through the branches, stories weave,
Of loss and love, of hearts that cleave,
The canvas rich, a tale begun,
Beneath the gaze of setting sun.

Secrets dwell in twilight's glow,
A narrative only the brave know,
In every color, dreams collide,
Underneath, where feelings bide.

So linger here, where beauty lies,
Beneath the shroud of sanguine skies,
For every end shall give you wings,
To dance among the sunset's wings.

Flickering Shadows on the Crimson Trail

Whispers dance beneath the moon,
As shadows play, a haunting tune.
Each rustle stirs the silent trees,
Awakens dreams upon the breeze.

Footsteps echo down the lane,
In the stillness, echoes reign.
Crimson leaves, they swirl and twirl,
Amongst the magic, they unfurl.

A lantern glows in twilight's grasp,
Where secrets hide and memories clasp.
Flickering softly, a guiding light,
Leading hearts through the velvet night.

With every sigh, the darkness sways,
The path unfolds in mystic ways.
A tapestry of stars above,
Weaving tales of lost true love.

So journey forth, with courage bright,
Through shadowed woods into the light.
For every flicker shows a trail,
Where dreams take flight on crimson sail.

Ethereal Glow Amidst the Edges of Night

In twilight's breath, soft light unfolds,
A shimmer cast on whispers bold.
The night, it cradles secrets deep,
Awakening dreams that softly seep.

Beneath the veil, the world does gleam,
A ghostly dance, a tender dream.
With every flick, the shadows sigh,
As stars ignite the vast, dark sky.

Ethereal glow, a beckoning spark,
Illuminates the silent dark.
Where time and magic intertwine,
And stardust drapes the ancient pine.

Through lingering moments, heartbeats race,
In every gleam, a sweet embrace.
Hold tight the light, let wonder flow,
As mystery blooms in night's tableau.

So wander through this velvet space,
Where whispers echo, shadows trace.
Embrace the glow, let spirits soar,
In the edges of night, forevermore.

Shattered Light on the Fiery Crown

A fiery crown upon the dawn,
Where shattered light bids night be gone.
Each hue a brush of warm delight,
Awakening dreams in morning's light.

Crimson skies and golden rays,
Herald the start of brand new days.
In whispered winds, the world awakes,
To greet the sun that softly breaks.

Through tangled branches, colors blend,
As shadows stretch, and moments mend.
A tapestry of warmth descends,
On all the hearts that nature tends.

Shattered light in vibrant shades,
A siren's call through forest glades.
Each sparkle sings the dawn's sweet song,
A reminder that we all belong.

So lift your gaze to skies above,
In every beam, find hope and love.
For in the light, the world is crowned,
With beauty etched, profound, unbound.

Nimbus of Red on the Breath of Dawn

A nimbus of red on morning's breath,
Where light and shadow dance with death.
Each moment whispers soft and clear,
A promise held, a hope sincere.

In the stillness, dreams align,
Bathed in hues of rose and wine.
The dawn unfolds, a vibrant show,
As warmth embraces, ebb and flow.

Through gentle veils of glowing haze,
We find the start of endless days.
Each heartbeat echoes in the air,
As nature stirs from slumber's lair.

Awakened hearts will rise anew,
With glorious skies of every hue.
In every ray, a story told,
Of love and life in shades of gold.

So breathe in deep, let worries fade,
Embrace the warmth that light has made.
For in this moment, all is right,
A nimbus glows upon the light.

Shimmering Crimson in Hidden Realms

In twilight's hush where shadows dance,
A shimmering crimson spark does glance.
Through hidden realms both bright and gray,
Secrets whispered in skies of clay.

The ancient woods, they breathe the night,
Each leaf aglow with soft, warm light.
Reflected dreams in still-lit streams,
A tapestry woven of starlit themes.

In corners where the faeries play,
Time is but an ebbing sway.
With laughter floating on the breeze,
The world awakens, hearts find ease.

Crimson blooms unearth their bliss,
In hidden glades, the stars' sweet kiss.
A path uncharted, bold, and bright,
Guides seekers through the heart of night.

Luminous Tracks of a Fallen Star

A flicker falls from heaven's seam,
A luminous track where wishes gleam.
Across the sky, the colors dance,
A fleeting moment, a lucky chance.

Where earth meets sky in twilight's arms,
The world enchants with its hidden charms.
Lost in the echoes of dreams untold,
The heart beats brave, the spirit bold.

With each soft whisper of the night,
Stars unlock their jeweled light.
The universe hums a soothing tune,
As dreams uplift beneath the moon.

So chase the trail of the fallen spark,
For every wish ignites the dark.
And in the silence, magic glows,
With hope renewing, as fortune flows.

Sanguine Dawn Beyond the Celestial Ridge

When dawn breaks soft beyond the ridge,
Sanguine hues ignite the bridge.
Where day and night in silence meet,
A symphony, both raw and sweet.

The hills awaken, kissed with light,
While dreams dissolve in morning's flight.
Each blossom sways to nature's tune,
Beneath the gaze of a silver moon.

In vibrant whispers on the breeze,
The world unfolds with gentle ease.
Colors merge in the morning glow,
A canvas wild, a tale to show.

The sanguine dawn, a bold embrace,
A tender touch, a warm, soft grace.
With open hearts, we greet the day,
And gratitude leads us on our way.

Resplendent Ashes of Forgotten Days

In twilight's grasp, where silence lays,
Resplendent ashes mark the days.
Each ember holds a story old,
Of laughter lost and dreams untold.

The fire flickers, memories spark,
In shadows deep, where whispers hark.
Time weaves gently through the past,
A tapestry of shadows cast.

Each flicker speaks of love's sweet grace,
Of longing held in warm embrace.
Yet in the ashes, hope remains,
A dance of joy, despite the pains.

Resplendent lives, though dimmed by night,
Still flicker soft with inner light.
For in each heart, a story waits,
To rise anew, despite the fates.

Red Mist Playing in the Twilight

In the soft haze of evening's breath,
Shadows dance where whispers tread,
A tapestry of secrets weaved,
In silence where the stories bled.

Crimson threads in twilight spun,
Dreams awaken, softly kissed,
Time stands still, as moments meld,
In the mist, the past exists.

Beneath the arch of fading light,
Bitter sweet the calls of night,
A shimmer in the foggy veil,
Promises made, heartbeats frail.

The echoes of the day retreat,
As stars emerge with twinkling eyes,
In this red mist, we find our fate,
Awakening the night's surprise.

And so we tread on peril's edge,
Through paths where shadows intertwine,
Each step a promise, every breath,
A journey penned by hands divine.

Horizon's Gloom and the Day's Return

When darkness leans on the horizon's crest,
A gloom that drapes the waking world,
The sun creeps forth, a daring guest,
With threads of gold, the dark unfurled.

Whispers cling to the morning dew,
As shadows fade in golden light,
Hope rekindles, the sky anew,
A dance of day to banish night.

In every corner, magic stirs,
As colors bloom, a lover's sigh,
The earth awakes as songbird purrs,
With melodies that lift us high.

Yet deep the gloom, its fingers trace,
The edges of our fleeting dreams,
But with each dawn, we find embrace,
In warmth of sun, our spirit beams.

So let the twilight softly wave,
And bow to night with grace and charm,
For in the dusk, the shadows pave,
The road of life, both kind and harm.

Dusk's Red Embrace on the Edge of Night

As day surrenders to dusk's red flame,
In whispers low, the land exhales,
Each shade of crimson knows our name,
With every breath, the twilight quails.

The horizon bleeds with fervent sighs,
While dreams, like fireflies, take flight,
Painting reveries in twilight skies,
A soft caress as day turns night.

Lights flicker in the distance vast,
A symphony of shadows calls,
In dusk's embrace, the day is cast,
A lingering peace before night falls.

With every heartbeat, whispers rise,
In the folds of dusk's gentle veil,
Secrets held in twilight's guise,
A world alive with many tales.

The sky ignites, the stars align,
In red's embrace, we find our way,
Through woven paths where fates entwine,
A journey carved from night to day.

Folklore Wrapped in Ethereal Glow

Once upon a time, the legends say,
In realms where shadows weave their tales,
Folklore wrapped in night's soft sway,
With lacing dreams like feathered veils.

The moonlight whispers secrets old,
In every breeze, a story's song,
Of heroes brave and hearts of gold,
In echoes where the ancients throng.

Ethereal glow enchants the night,
With shimmering threads of fate and hope,
A dance of wishes, soft and bright,
In starlit dreams where spirits cope.

So listen close, as shadows hum,
For every heart that dares to soar,
Holds within the lullabies of some,
A tale of love, forevermore.

Through darkened woods and winding paths,
We wander in the grace of lore,
In every breath, the magic lasts,
As we embrace what dreams restore.

Ember Tides on the Frontier of Dreams

The twilight whispers secrets low,
While ember tides begin to glow.
In dreams we sail on starlit streams,
With boats of hope and woven dreams.

A misty shore where shadows play,
Each wave can wash the fears away.
As night unfolds its velvet arms,
We drift through magic, safe from harms.

The perfume of the distant pine,
Guides lost souls to the edge of time.
With lanterns lit, we trace the way,
On shimmering paths at break of day.

The frontier stretches, wild and wide,
With dreams as gifts, the stars our guide.
Together we shall chart this flight,
Ember tides, our hearts ignite.

And when the dawn begins to creep,
We'll hold the night in memory's keep.
For in those dreams, where shadows blend,
The ember tides shall never end.

Mirrored Flames in Still Waters

In still waters, a truth unsaid,
Mirrored flames where dreams are fed.
Reflections dance in cosmic light,
Whispers of magic spark the night.

The flickering glow weaves tales untold,
Of bravery fierce and hearts bold.
Each wave carries a whispered name,
In the stillness, sparks of flame.

The surface shimmers, secrets deep,
Holding wishes that fate shall keep.
We cast our hopes on currents wide,
In mirrored flames, we take our stride.

With every ripple, a story flows,
As the evening's gentle breeze blows.
Time will bend, with hearts entwined,
In still waters, our fates aligned.

So let us sail on this quiet sea,
Where flames reflect our destiny.
In mirrored dreams, we ignite our hearts,
In the stillness, the magic starts.

Searing Veil Over Silent Summits

Beneath the stars, on silent peaks,
A searing veil of mystery speaks.
The night sky shimmers with ancient lore,
As dreams unfold beyond the door.

In shadows deep, the mountains sigh,
With whispers of those who dare to fly.
The air is thick with secrets' call,
On summits high, we embrace it all.

The fire within ignites our soul,
A journey carved, a whispered goal.
Through valleys dark, we find our light,
With searing veils, we take our flight.

The silent summits guard their grace,
A sacred dance, a timeless space.
As dawn approaches, we boldy stand,
With hearts united, hand in hand.

In searing rays, the truth shall shine,
Over silent peaks, our spirits entwine.
With courage fierce, we'll reach the skies,
And toward forever, our hopes shall rise.

Dawn's Flicker Behind the Ashen Veil

Behind the veil, where ashes lie,
Dawn's flicker whispers soft goodbyes.
A gentle promise, sweet and bright,
Awakens dreams in morning light.

The world adorned in shades of gray,
Yearns for the sun to pierce the fray.
With every breath, a spark ignites,
In hearts reborn, igniting sights.

The ashen veil, a canvas wide,
Hides below the colors that bide.
For in this hush, new wonders grow,
As dawn commands the shadows low.

Through fusion of the night and day,
We find our path in twilight's sway.
As golden rays slip through the seams,
Dawn's flicker fuels our cherished dreams.

So let us rise on wings of fire,
Embracing hope, our hearts aspire.
In every flicker, life shall soar,
Behind the veil, we seek for more.

A Tapestry of Warmth and Wellness

In the hearth's gentle glow, we gather near,
Whispers of comfort, a message clear.
Soft laughter dances in the twilight air,
Hearts intertwined, free from despair.

Embers crackle, a soothing song,
Together we thrive, where we belong.
In moments shared, we weave our thread,
A tapestry bright, where love is spread.

With every smile, a promise we weave,
In the fabric of life, we believe.
Morning light spills on our dreams anew,
A world of wonders, just waiting for you.

Through trials we face, hand in hand,
In this sacred space, we boldly stand.
Here's to the warmth that always surrounds,
A symphony sweet, in joyful sounds.

As seasons shift, and shadows play,
Together we flourish, come what may.
In the tapestry's weave, a glorious tale,
Of warmth and wellness, we shall prevail.

Resonance of Light Within the Shadows

In the quiet corners where secrets dwell,
Soft glimmers of hope break through the shell.
Whispers of courage, in darkness reside,
A spark of light, impossible to hide.

Through meridian paths where shadows creep,
Dreamers awaken, their visions deep.
With every breath, the echoes resound,
Love's gentle touch can always be found.

In twilight's embrace, the night sings low,
Radiance dwells where the heart dares to go.
Forging connections, like stars in the sky,
Each flicker a tale, as the night drifts by.

The dance of the moon, a silvery guide,
Illuminates hope, where sorrows abide.
In the depths of the night, soft shadows will sway,
A harmony perfect, come what may.

As dawn gently breaks, the shadows will fade,
The resonance strong, our fears unmade.
Together we find the light in the dark,
In every heartbeat, we ignite the spark.

The Awakening of Ruins in Reddish Veils

Amidst crumbled stones, where echoes remain,
Whispers of history call out in vain.
The dusk wraps her shawl, a reddish hue,
Awakening life in the shadows anew.

Forgotten tales linger through time's embrace,
In shadows and light, each silence we trace.
The heart of the earth, in stories untold,
In ruins we find treasures of old.

A dance with the past in this twilight glow,
Resurrecting dreams that once long ago.
With every step, the silence will sing,
A symphony lush in the whispers of spring.

Through weathered arches, the past finds its voice,
Inviting our hearts to ponder, rejoice.
What once lay in silence can rise from the dust,
In the ruins, we gather, we learn, and we trust.

As the day fades, a canvas is drawn,
In reddish veils of an exquisite dawn.
We unearth lives that have come and have gone,
In the art of remembrance, we find our song.

Sweet Lament of the Incandescent Dawn

In the hushed embrace of the early morn,
Life stirs awake, with the softest yawn.
A canvas of colors, a gentle art,
In hues of gold, it ignites the heart.

As sunlight spills over the sleeping trees,
The world breathes out, carried by the breeze.
Each bloom unfolds with a fragrant sigh,
Whispers of hope in the azure sky.

Yet in this beauty, a sorrow may dwell,
For moments once cherished, we bid farewell.
The fleeting day dawns, resplendent, bright,
In its incandescent glow, we find our light.

Through nostalgia's lens, we cherish our past,
In remembering love that will always last.
Yet here in the dawn, we are given the chance,
To dance with the shadows, to dream, to advance.

So let us embrace this sweet lament,
For in every dawn, our spirits are sent.
Through the veil of the night, we've traveled far,
In the incandescent dawn, we shine like a star.

Twilight Mist Wrapping Fiery Wings

In twilight's mist, the shadows dance,
With fiery wings that spin and prance.
Whispers float on the evening air,
A magic spell woven with care.

Crimson hues in the fading light,
Embrace the stars that twinkle bright.
Heralds of night in a soft serenade,
In this world where dreams are made.

Beneath the arch of the dusky sky,
Creatures of wonder flit on high.
They glide through clouds of whispering gray,
In twilight's mist, they waltz and sway.

Hope takes flight on gossamer wings,
Through tangled branches, the nightbird sings.
Each note a promise, each tune a plea,
In this twilight realm, wild and free.

So let the dusk wrap us in its fold,
With tales of adventure waiting to be told.
In twilight's mist, our spirits will soar,
Embracing the magic forevermore.

Ruby Whisper in Ethereal Skies

In the canvas of dusk, a ruby hue,
Whispers of love born anew.
Ethereal skies dance with delight,
As stars awaken to grace the night.

Dreamy landscapes stretch across the sea,
Painting the world with vibrant glee.
Each breeze a secret, softly conveyed,
In the twilight glow, dreams aren't delayed.

Softly twinkling, the heavens embrace,
Beneath their gaze, we quicken our pace.
With laughter rising like whispers of fire,
Together, we chase our hearts' desire.

Veils of night unfurl like a spell,
In the embrace of shadows, we dwell.
Each ruby whisper, a tender decree,
Binding our fates in celestial glee.

As the moon cradles the sighing wind,
In ethereal skies, magic begins.
With brave hearts entwined in the cosmic waltz,
We find our way, void of all faults.

Glowing Haze Amidst the Summit's Call

In the glowing haze, the world feels near,
Whispers of mountains, crisp and clear.
Summit's call echoes in the night,
Guiding lost souls towards the light.

Every step taken, a story unfolds,
Of ancient glories and dreams untold.
Amidst the pines, where shadows play,
The heart finds peace, come what may.

With every breath, the silence sings,
The air alive with enchanted things.
In the glowing haze, our spirits roam,
Finding strength in this sacred home.

Crystals glisten, adorned in frost,
In this realm, no moments are lost.
As we stand tall, hearts intertwined,
Summit's call, a promise divined.

Together we rise, hand in hand,
In the soft embrace of this timeless land.
For in the glowing haze, we uncover our fate,
Bound by the mountains, forever elate.

Flare of Dawn in the Gloaming Dusk

As dawn unfurls its golden breath,
Awakening life from the grasp of death.
Flare of light in the gloaming mist,
Kissing the shadows, the night's soft tryst.

Rays of sunshine dance on dew-kissed leaves,
Filling the world with hope that believes.
Birds sing sweetly, a morning's embrace,
In the soft light, we find our place.

Colors swirl in a vibrant parade,
Each hue a story, one never betrayed.
The sky ignites in a glorious hue,
As dreams take flight, born anew.

In the hush of dawn, the world holds its breath,
A moment suspended between life and death.
Flare of hope as the sun breaks through,
In the quiet stillness, the universe grew.

For in every dawn lies a chance to start,
With the flame of life igniting the heart.
In the gloaming dusk, we find our way,
With the promise of light, heralding day.

Scarlet Horizon in the Whispering Pines

Beneath the boughs, the shadows dance,
Whispers of magic in a gentle trance.
Crimson hues stretch far and wide,
Where secrets in the twilight abide.

The pines stand tall, with stories to tell,
Of travelers lost in their enchanted spell.
As day gives way to the night's embrace,
Stars awaken in the velvet space.

A breeze carries the tales of old,
Of hearts once brave and spirits bold.
In this realm where time unwinds,
The scarlet horizon softly finds.

Each flicker of light, a promise made,
In this sanctuary, fears do fade.
With every heartbeat, the world takes flight,
In the whispering sands of the coming night.

Last Light on the Fiery Ridge

Upon the ridge, the sunsets gleam,
A symphony wrapped in a golden dream.
The sky ablaze, with colors that blend,
Where the dusk whispers, and shadows descend.

Mountains stand watch, ancient and wise,
As the sun dips low, painting the skies.
Each moment a treasure, a fleeting delight,
The last light dances, bidding goodnight.

Crickets begin their sweet serenade,
While secrets of twilight effortlessly cascade.
In the fading glow, hearts softly sigh,
Embracing the twilight as time slips by.

The ridge holds its breath in reverent pause,
Capturing magic without a cause.
In the horizon's glow, stories reside,
The last light whispers from the fiery ridge.

Morning Gleam Through Ruby Veils

When dawn breaks through with tender grace,
The world awakes in a warm embrace.
Ruby veils lift, unveiling the day,
Sunbeams dance in a joyous sway.

Bud and bloom in a vibrant show,
Nature's canvas, where colors flow.
A chorus of birds, a welcome song,
Echoes of morning, vibrant and strong.

The softest breeze chases dreams afar,
Weaving hope beneath the morning star.
With every glimmer, a brand-new chance,
In the light of dawn, all hearts advance.

Each ray a promise of wonders near,
A world reformed, so fresh and clear.
Through ruby veils, the magic gleams,
In the embrace of morning dreams.

Glint of Blood in a Sea of Gray

In twilight shadows, the silence reigns,
A haunting echo of bittersweet pains.
Beneath the clouds, so heavy and low,
A glint of blood in the undertow.

Ghostly whispers, the past once bold,
Tales of sorrow, now softly told.
In each heartbeat, a flicker of fire,
What once was hope now treads on wire.

Yet through the gray, a shimmer breaks,
A sign of life as the darkness quakes.
For even in gloom, rebirth may rise,
From ashes and ruins, hope never dies.

So let the shadows speak of the fight,
The glint of blood a testament bright.
In a sea of gray where dreams may sway,
Life finds a way, come what may.

Silent Wings of a Scarlet Dream

In the hush of the night, they soar,
Carrying whispers of secret lore.
Crimson feathers glide through air,
A dance of destiny, light and rare.

Softly they weave through shadows deep,
Guardians of dreams, as we sleep.
Moments unfurl in silent grace,
A tapestry spun in a timeless space.

Echoes of laughter, faint and near,
Carried by winds, for the heart to hear.
The world aglow in shades of red,
As visions awaken, our spirits spread.

With gentle sighs, they kiss the ground,
Where hopes and wishes are tightly bound.
In the painted sky, a spark ignites,
Guiding our souls through the endless nights.

In the glow of a soft, warm dream,
Boundless worlds begin to gleam.
So let us follow where they lead,
On silent wings, our hearts uncreed.

Radiance Lost in Veils of Darkness

Beneath the shroud of midnight's cloak,
Where shadows whisper and silence spoke.
Flickering flames, they dance and sway,
A battle fought for the light of day.

Ghostly figures flit in despair,
Scattered like leaves caught in the air.
The echoes of laughter, dulled and faint,
As hope retreats, a weary saint.

Stars entwined in a web of gloom,
A haunting melody fills the room.
Each heartbeat echoes through the night,
In search of the lost, the fading light.

But from the depths, a glimmer fights,
Breaking through the thickest nights.
With weary eyes, we yearn to see,
The radiance that sets spirits free.

So rise again, let dreams unfold,
In the arms of the brave and bold.
For from the darkness, dawn will break,
In radiant hues, our hearts awake.

Fiery Sighs Beneath Starlit Skies

Beneath the heavens' infinite gaze,
Where dreams are woven in fiery blaze.
A sigh escapes on the evening air,
Lost and yearning, forever rare.

The stars, they shimmer like secrets kept,
In silent beauty, while mortals slept.
A tapestry of wishes, wild and free,
Each one a glimpse of what could be.

Through swirling clouds, the embers dance,
With every sigh, a fleeting chance.
The night cradles our tender fears,
As laughter mingles with unshed tears.

Yet in the darkness, a spark ignites,
A promise of warmth in colder nights.
For through the sighs of longing hearts,
A fiery glow, a new dawn starts.

With each whisper of the waking dawn,
We rise to meet the light that's drawn.
In starlit skies, our spirits rise,
With fiery sighs and endless ties.

Twilight's Blood on the Frozen Heights

Upon the peaks where eagles dare,
Twilight spills its secrets rare.
A crimson hue stains the purest snow,
In the stillness, whispers flow.

The chill of night wraps tight and swings,
As nature sings of forgotten things.
With frozen breaths, the silence weaves,
Stories held in the bated leaves.

A tapestry of dusk and dawn,
Where shadows linger, and dreams are drawn.
Twilight's blood flows, a solemn sight,
Kissing the earth, as day turns night.

Yet from the heights, a phoenix cries,
Awakening hope beneath darkening skies.
With every heartbeat, a soul yearns free,
For with the twilight, the end can be.

So let us climb, to the frozen heights,
Where dreams awaken in endless flights.
Embracing the dusk, with hearts aglow,
In twilight's blood, our spirits grow.

Blazing Veil Across the Horizon

The sun ignites the azure sky,
A blazing veil that whispers high,
In hues of gold and crimson bright,
It dances forth, a wondrous sight.

Beneath the flames, the shadows creep,
Awakening the world from sleep,
Each ember tells a tale of yore,
Of battles fought and ancient lore.

As twilight fades, the colors bleed,
Crimson hues of a heart's deep need,
They bind the earth and sky above,
A tapestry of loss and love.

The horizon's edge, a blazing seam,
Where dreams ignite and children dream,
In twilight whispers, secrets sway,
And promise dawn through night's dismay.

In every flicker, a spark remains,
Of laughter lost and bittersweet chains,
So let us stand, eyes on that fire,
Embrace the veil, our hearts conspire.

Luminous Smoke in the Valley's Embrace

Across the valley's gentle slope,
A fog drifts in, a silken rope,
It curls around the trees so tall,
In whispers soft, it starts to call.

The air is rich with stories spun,
Of lost horizons, battles won,
Each wisp of smoke a tale retold,
Of bravery, both fierce and bold.

As twilight weaves its twilight threads,
The luminous smoke in silence spreads,
It blankets all in a misty shroud,
Like secrets kept, away from the crowd.

The stars peek through with distant grace,
As moonlight bathes this sacred space,
Within the fog, a dream awakes,
Where shadows stir and magic breaks.

In this embrace, we wander free,
Held by the night's soft mystery,
We roam the valley, hand in hand,
In luminous smoke, we take our stand.

Reddish Haze Cloaked in Old Legends

In the twilight's fading breath,
A reddish haze, a tale of death,
Cloaked in legends of yesterdays,
Where shadows linger and silence pays.

The fireflies twinkle like lost dreams,
In eldritch light, a world of schemes,
Each whispered word a fragment spun,
Of ancient quests and battles won.

Beyond the hills, the echoes call,
Of heroes' rise, and destined fall,
In every glow, a story weaves,
Of wisdom gained, and hearts that grieve.

As night descends in crimson hues,
The stars reveal the path we choose,
In this haze, we seek our fate,
With courage fierce and hearts elate.

To tread the legends, brave and bold,
In reddish haze, their truths unfold,
With every step, we claim our name,
In echoes whispered, we find the flame.

Fire and Mist: Chronicles of the Sky

In skies where fire meets the mist,
A dance of elements, a fateful tryst,
The clouds engulf the fiery glow,
In fleeting moments, time moves slow.

The winds converge with fierce delight,
A rhapsody of day and night,
The thunder rolls, the lightning strikes,
In this wild dance, the earth it hikes.

Glimmers shine like scattered dreams,
Through raging storms and sunlit beams,
Each breath of wind a story earned,
Of worlds colliding, lessons learned.

The fire's warmth, the misty chill,
Both entwined with iron will,
In this ballet of heavens high,
We write our own chronicles in the sky.

So let us journey, hearts aglow,
Through fire and mist, where legends flow,
For every tale that stirs the air,
Is one we hold, beyond compare.

Glowing Labyrinth of Fading Light

In the winding paths of silver haze,
Whispers of magic dance and sway.
Lost within the shimmering maze,
Shadows flicker, fading away.

Secrets murmur in the night,
Echoes of dreams, forgotten tales.
Each turn reveals a glimmering sight,
As hope prevails where darkness pales.

Twilight's embrace, a gentle sigh,
Stars awaken, one by one.
Guiding the lost with a soft cry,
Leading them home before the sun.

Through the labyrinth, hearts entwined,
Braving the unknown with a spark.
In every corner, treasures find,
As hope ignites the endless dark.

At the journey's end, what's viewed,
A world transformed, aglow with grace.
In this haven, souls renewed,
Together we stand, face to face.

Red Whispers Over the Shadowed Valleys

Beneath the crimson, twilight's spell,
Whispers travel through the trees.
Tales of longing begin to swell,
On the soft breeze, secrets tease.

Over valleys cloaked in night,
Echoes linger, faint and deep.
Crimson shadows paint the light,
As the weary world drifts to sleep.

Amidst the rustling of the leaves,
Footsteps tread on ancient ground.
Every heartbeat softly weaves,
Stories of love that once were found.

In the stillness, hearts conspire,
To reclaim what time forgot.
With every sigh, they spark a fire,
In the dusk where hope is sought.

With the dawn, the colors will change,
But the whispers linger on.
In the transformation, nothing's strange,
For in love's light, we'll carry on.

Elysian Flames Beneath the Veiled Dawn

In the shimmer of a new day's light,
Elysian flames begin to rise.
Veils of dawn, so pure and bright,
Paint the sky with whispered sighs.

Every shadow, now aglow,
Beneath the warmth of sunlight's grace.
Fading echoes of long ago,
Merge with dreams in a tender embrace.

From glimmers born of hope and fire,
Souls awaken in morning's breath.
Chasing passions, heart's desire,
Finding life where once was death.

Together we stand, side by side,
Unfolding futures, bright and clear.
In the glow where dreams abide,
We soar above, casting out fear.

As the world turns, fate will weave,
A tapestry of colors grand.
In this moment, we believe,
In the magic of a well-lit land.

Glistening Twilight in the Valley's Grasp

In the valley's heart where twilight gleams,
Soft hues blend in tender sway.
Echoes of hopes and fleeting dreams,
Dance along the edge of day.

Stars awaken with twinkling eyes,
Dotting the canvas of the night.
Where the earth and sky softly sighs,
In the glow, all feels just right.

Every shadow holds a story,
Whispered secrets, lost and found.
In their depths lie moments of glory,
As silence wraps us all around.

Nature sings, a soothing tune,
In the gentle caress of the breeze.
A symphony ends, yet starts anew,
With the promise of sweet melodies.

In this twilight, hearts awaken,
Embracing all that life can bring.
Fears undone, never forsaken,
In this moment, together we sing.

Vestiges of Fire in the Veiled Horizon

In twilight's grasp, the embers glow,
Whispers of heat where cool winds blow.
Flickers dance on the edge of night,
Dreams of flame in the fading light.

Beneath the arch of a star-studded sky,
Secrets of warmth, they gently sigh.
Vapor trails of a bygone spark,
Hope ignites in the lingering dark.

Through shadows deep, the memories play,
Fading echoes of a once bright day.
On horizon's crest, a promise bold,
Stories of fire in whispers told.

Each flicker holds a tale to share,
Of laughter, loss, the weight of care.
In the veils of dusk, their colors blend,
Paths of the heart that never end.

So let the firelight guide our way,
Through verdant fields where shadows sway.
With every spark, a journey's start,
Inflamed with love, a burning heart.

Crimson Veil Over Ashen Peaks

Across the mountains, a shroud of red,
Crimson whispers where the dreamers tread.
Veils of dusk caress the ancient stone,
Fables of love in the wind are sown.

With every shadow that dances near,
Brighter the hope that banishes fear.
Ashen peaks in glimmering light,
Tales of courage reclaim the night.

Each echo of a long-lost song,
Calls to the heart where we belong.
A tapestry woven of fate and fire,
Dreams that ascend, ever higher.

Hold on to warmth in the chill of doubt,
Crimson promises the soul about.
In twilight's arms, we find our grace,
Each shimmering moment a sacred space.

Beneath the veil, the fires remember,
Moments of joy in the heart of November.
With each ascent, we find our call,
Crimson flames that shall never fall.

Embered Haze in Celestial Rise

From ashes born, the glow anew,
Embers beckon with warmth so true.
In starlit skies, the shadows gleam,
A world aglow, wrapped in a dream.

With each dawn, the haze unfurls,
Whirls of magic in vibrant swirls.
The lonely hearts and kindred souls,
Captured in light as the universe rolls.

In whispered winds, they tell their tale,
Of burning passion and love's prevail.
Celestial rise, where dreams ascend,
Hearts entwined in an endless blend.

Each ember whispers of hope's embrace,
Waking the stars in a boundless space.
Through crispy leaves, the echoes tease,
The warmth of fire, the kiss of breeze.

Yet in the haze, we feel the chill,
Memories linger, hearts to fill.
Embered glow in the morning mist,
Promises held in a lover's tryst.

Scarlet Shroud on the Mountain's Edge

Upon the crest where the wild winds weep,
A scarlet shroud where shadows creep.
In whispers soft, the mountains sigh,
Secrets woven in the twilight sky.

With twilight's brush, the horizon stains,
Nature's canvas where passion reigns.
Each breath of wind, a lover's vow,
Crimson reminders of the here and now.

Through every heart, a melody flows,
In the depths of night, where the wild rose grows.
Mountain's edge, a place of dreams,
Caught in the moonlight's gentle beams.

Scarlet shadows in the fading glow,
Embers whisper what we long to know.
Tales of old in the quiet air,
Kisses of time that linger there.

So journey forth, where courage blends,
In the scarlet glow, where time transcends.
Each step resounds in the heart's parade,
On mountain's edge, love will not fade.

Vermilion Veils of a Rising Sun

In the morning glow, shadows retreat,
Whispers of dawn on dew-kissed grass.
Vermilion veils where day and night meet,
Promises linger, as moments pass.

Breezes awaken the sleeping trees,
Their leaves dance gently with eager grace.
The world stirs softly, the heart finds ease,
A wondrous sight, a magical place.

Mountains blush under the sun's embrace,
Crimson horizons awake from dreams.
Nature unfolds with exquisite pace,
Life unfolds in kaleidoscope themes.

Birds take flight in a symphony sung,
Songs of the morn fill the vibrant air.
In every note, the heart is young,
A tapestry woven with love and care.

With every hue, a tale begins,
Vermilion threads in time's great loom.
In the warm light, the past rescinds,
Hope blooms wide in the morning's bloom.

Radiant Cloud Over Charred Heights

Over the peaks where embers die,
A radiant cloud drapes in sorrow's shroud.
Echoes of flames still linger nigh,
Yet hope shines bright, undeterred, unbowed.

Silent whispers of the forest grieve,
Yet new growth sprouts from ashes old.
In each small bud, a tale to weave,
Nature's strength, a sight to behold.

Golden sunbeams break through the haze,
Painting the land with soft, warm light.
In this moment, the heart ablaze,
Resilience found in the face of night.

Above charred heights, the sky unfurls,
A canvas alive with colors bold.
From the dark earth, new wonder swirls,
Life's promise unbroken, stories told.

In shadows cast by the high retreat,
Radiant dreams begin to take flight.
In every heartbeat, in every beat,
Hope finds a way to transform the night.

Sanguine Mist Embracing the Dawn

A sanguine mist drapes the fields in peace,
Soft breaths of morning, like secrets shared.
The night withdraws, its grip released,
Each fragile moment, tenderly spared.

Through veils of fog, the world awakens,
Colors bleed softly in muted hues.
Nature's heart, in silence, quickens,
Frankincense whispers of morning's muse.

Fields of blooms in red and gold rise,
Whispers of promise, the sun's caress.
In this embrace where beauty lies,
The spirit finds solace in nature's dress.

Every droplet glistens like dreams,
Hope reflected in the quiet streams.
As dawn unfurls its painted seams,
The world ignites with radiant beams.

Within this embrace of mist and light,
Sanguine dreams beckon hearts to mend.
In every sigh, the day feels right,
Life's journey weaves, a timeless blend.

Aurora of Red-Flecked Dreams

Beneath the sky, a festival glows,
An aurora dances with vibrant glee.
Threads of red in the twilight flows,
Dreams awaken, as wild and free.

Mystic shapes in the evening air,
Fingers of light that touch the ground.
In this enchantment, fervent prayer,
Hearts entwined, forever bound.

Whispers of stardust kiss the night,
Each flicker holds tales yet to be told.
In dreams of red, the spirit takes flight,
A tapestry of wonders, rich and bold.

For in the depth of twilight's hue,
Every heartbeat mimics the stars' song.
An aurora's glow, a dance anew,
In this moment, we all belong.

With every breath, new hopes ignite,
Red-flecked dreams will always gleam.
In the night's embrace, pure delight,
Life unfolds like a beautiful dream.

Amber Dreams in the Wake of Fire

In the twilight's gentle embrace,
Amber embers whisper low,
Dreams dance like flickering stars,
Woven in the warm, soft glow.

Beneath the boughs of ancient trees,
Golden whispers weave their tales,
A symphony of fleeting breath,
As night's cool mist gently prevails.

Mystic echoes fill the air,
Winds carry songs from afar,
Firelight paints the shadows deep,
Guided by the evening star.

With each sparkle, a story told,
In the hush, secrets reside,
Amber dreams of hopes reborn,
In the warmth of love's bright tide.

Beneath the moon's watchful eye,
Hearts ignite with ancient fire,
In the wake of night's embrace,
We reclaim our lost desire.

Whispering Flames of Distant Shores

On the edge of silver waves,
Whispers rise like gentle sighs,
Flames of hope on distant shores,
Underneath expansive skies.

Each flicker tells a tale of yore,
Where starlit nights and dreams collide,
With flames that dance in joyful glee,
Chasing shadows, turning tides.

Ancient lullabies they weave,
Carried forth by winds of fate,
Every ember holds a promise,
As they flicker, love creates.

In the darkness, visions shimmer,
Flames revealing golden years,
Whispering secrets like the sea,
Telling tales that dry our tears.

From the shores, our voices rise,
In harmony, we find our core,
Together with the whispering flames,
Igniting dreams on distant shores.

Eclipsed Radiance of the Dying Day

As daylight fades to twilight's kiss,
Eclipsed by shadows that softly creep,
Radiance lingers on the brink,
A fleeting moment before we sleep.

The horizon bleeds with hues so bold,
Gold and crimson blend in flight,
While day plays hide and seek with night,
Wrapping the world in a velvet light.

Each petal trembles in the breeze,
Stories woven in twilight's glow,
Dancing fragments of long-lost days,
In the hush where memories grow.

Time unravels within this frame,
As the dusk holds whispers of what was,
In the eclipse of day's soft breath,
We gather what the heart still loves.

Underneath the shroud of stars,
We find solace in the gray,
Cradled in the arms of night,
Releasing dreams at dying day.

Ghostly Lights in the Embered Woods

In the woods where shadows tread,
Ghostly lights begin to dance,
Echoes of the past arise,
In the stillness, the heart's romance.

Flickering whispers, soft and low,
Guide the wanderers lost in thought,
Illuminating ancient paths,
Mapping dreams that time forgot.

Beneath the boughs, where secrets hide,
Each glimmer tells of lives once lived,
Fragile threads of fate entwined,
In these woods where spirits give.

A tapestry of twilight's song,
Ghostly lights weave through the trees,
Leading hearts to their true home,
In the whispering, unseen breeze.

With every step, a promise made,
In the embered woods we roam,
Held in night's embrace of dreams,
These ghostly lights guide us home.

Radiant Haze at Daybreak's Call

The sun peeks shyly, softly bright,
A hazy glow, a gentle light.
Whispers dance through waking trees,
In morning's breath, the world is at ease.

Birds take flight on shimmering air,
Their songs of joy, a sweetened prayer.
Golden rays on dew-kissed grass,
A fleeting moment, here to pass.

Clouds like dreams stretch wide and free,
Painting tales for all to see.
In this dawn's embrace we find,
A magic woven, intertwined.

The sky blushes in hues so gay,
As night retreats, chased away.
Each heartbeat thrums, a rhythmic thrall,
In radiant haze at daybreak's call.

Let time stand still, let echoes play,
In this bright dawn, come what may.
For in the light, all shadows fade,
In brilliant colors, dreams are made.

Threads of Red in the Morning Light

Crimson threads adorn the sky,
As daylight bids the stars goodbye.
With each stroke of the brush divine,
The world awakens, a grand design.

Silhouettes dance against the hue,
Nature's wonders, fresh and new.
Horizon glows with fiery might,
In threads of red, a pure delight.

Beneath the warmth, the shadows rest,
In whispered tones, the dawn is blessed.
Each petal opens, bold and bright,
To greet the sun's warm, golden light.

Fields of clover sway in grace,
As morning paints a vibrant face.
With laughter ringing in the air,
Threads of red, a love affair.

So let your heart in wonder soar,
For every day brings something more.
In vibrant hues, life's truth ignites,
With threads of red in morning's light.

Ashen Embers in a Celestial Embrace

In twilight's grasp, the shadows creep,
As ashen embers gently weep.
The fading glow of day's last breath,
Whispers tales of quiet death.

Stars awaken, a shimmering veil,
Their silver light, a haunting tale.
In this embrace, the night unfolds,
With secrets kept and dreams retold.

The moon, a guardian in the dark,
Sends shimmering rays, a silken spark.
In celestial dance, the worlds conjoin,
As ashen embers, hearts entwine.

With every sigh, the night grows deep,
In dreaming fields where shadows sleep.
The universe whispers in tones of grace,
In ashen embers, we find our place.

For in this stillness, calm and wise,
We glimpse the truth beneath the skies.
In the night's embrace, we shan't replace,
The warmth of love in cosmic space.

Misty Reveries of Fiery Rebirth

In morning mist, where dreams reside,
A world reborn, with hope as guide.
The fog blankets the earth with care,
In misty dreams of what we share.

The sun, a painter, bold and bright,
Brushes golden rays on misty white.
From slumber's grasp, the shadows rise,
To greet the dawn with sparkling eyes.

Each droplet glimmers, a crystal tear,
A sign of life, a promise near.
In fiery rebirth, the past does mend,
As misty whispers weave and bend.

With every breath, the world awakes,
In vibrant hues that nature makes.
The cycle spins, eternal fate,
In misty reveries, we celebrate.

Hold close the fire, let it ignite,
Your spirit soar beyond the night.
For in the dawn, our hearts reaffirm,
In misty dreams, we rise and churn.

Scarlet Echoes in the Fabric of Night

In twilight's hush, a whisper glows,
Secrets dance where the moonlight flows.
Shadows weave in crimson threads,
A tapestry where dreamers tread.

With each heartbeat, the stars ignite,
Filling the void with their soft light.
Echoes linger, sweet and rare,
A melody carried on the air.

Beneath the boughs, the night unfolds,
Stories whispered, softly told.
Fate entwined in a scarlet seam,
Woven in the fabric of a dream.

The nightingale sings a lullaby,
As wonders drift across the sky.
In the warmth of twilight's embrace,
Time meanders, a gentle pace.

So linger here, let worries cease,
In the echoes find your peace.
For in this realm where shadows play,
Night's scarlet magic gently sways.

Ashen Dust and Glowing Reflections

In twilight's glow, old embers fade,
Whispers of dreams in shadows laid.
Ashen dust swirls in the air,
Secrets breathe, both dark and rare.

Glistening hopes on a silver lake,
Reflections cast for the soul's sake.
Within the stillness, echoes call,
Find the strength to rise or fall.

Time trickles like golden sand,
Moments held in a gentle hand.
Each heartbeat whispers tales anew,
The past and present blend in view.

Amidst the quietude, voices sing,
Of what the dawn and dusk may bring.
Glowing thoughts take flight on wings,
In the heart, where the spirit clings.

So walk along this dusky trail,
Where ashen paths weave the tale.
Let glowing reflections guide your way,
Through shadows into the break of day.

Celestial Fire in the Forgotten East

In the grip of twilight's shroud,
Celestial fires dance unbowed.
Forgotten stories paint the sky,
As shimmering flames flicker high.

Whispers rise from ancient stones,
Echoes soft, in hushed tones.
Each spark a memory, fierce and bright,
Igniting the dreams hidden from sight.

The east awaits with open arms,
Embracing souls with its charms.
Fires flicker in the cool night air,
Inviting hearts to cast aside care.

Beneath the stars, time intertwines,
Life's rich tapestry brightly shines.
Celestial gates in shades of gold,
Tall tales of the brave and bold.

So wander forth, let your spirit soar,
Where the night reveals ancient lore.
Celestial fires will guide your quest,
In the forgotten east, you'll find your rest.

Veiled Horizons of Blushing Skies

As dawn unfolds in rosy light,
Veiled horizons greet the night.
Blush of day spills forth with grace,
Illuminating a dreaming place.

The clouds, adorned in softest hues,
Carry whispers of morning's muse.
Each breath a promise, fresh and pure,
In the stillness, hearts can stir.

Meridian dreams in silken threads,
Stitching stories as night treads.
The sun ascends, a beacon bright,
Awakening worlds in golden light.

With every murmur of the breeze,
Nature dances, swaying trees.
A symphony of colors blend,
In this realm where worries mend.

So linger long, on this divine,
In blushing skies, let spirits shine.
For with each dawn, new hopes arise,
In the embrace of veiled horizons lies.

Crimson Mist Over Ashen Dawn

A crimson mist envelops night,
As shadows stretch with fading light.
The world awakens, soft and shy,
Underneath a painted sky.

Whispers of the morning dew,
Embrace the earth in gentle hue.
Each blade of grass now gleams anew,
Beneath the sun, a brighter view.

The echoes of a dream still dance,
In the stillness, a fleeting chance.
Birds take flight in joyous prance,
As life unfolds, a waking romance.

Through deepened woods, the sunlight weaves,
A tapestry of gold and leaves.
The promise of a day that breathes,
Awakens hope and gently cleaves.

As shadows melt, the day is bright,
In every corner, pure delight.
Embrace the dawn, hold it tight,
For in its warmth, we find our light.

Ember Veils in a Rising Sun

Ember veils across the morn,
Softly through the shadows worn.
A fiery glow begins to rise,
Painting dreams across the skies.

Each flicker sings of tales untold,
Of hearts that brave the bitter cold.
In every spark, a wish resides,
In every heartbeat, hope abides.

The sun ascends, a golden sphere,
Casting warmth; it draws us near.
With open arms, the world awakes,
To find the joy that morning makes.

A dance of light upon the ground,
With every step, a joyful sound.
The whispers of the breezes sway,
To greet the promise of the day.

Through ember veils, new dreams ignite,
In every heart, a source of light.
The past dissolves, the future's spun,
As magic brews with rising sun.

Shadows Dance in Scarlet Haze

Shadows dance in scarlet haze,
Twilight weaves its mystic maze.
In whispered notes of soft despair,
The night unfolds with gentle care.

A flicker here, a glimmer there,
In moonlit beams, dreams fill the air.
With every step, a secret shared,
While starlit paths lead hearts prepared.

The world beneath, a slumber deep,
As silent winds begin to creep.
In twilight's arms, our fears dissolve,
As shadows twirl and night evolves.

Each breath a promise, held with grace,
In this enchanted, sacred space.
Through scarlet hues, our spirits rise,
To chase the stars beyond the skies.

In shadows' cloak, we find the way,
Through tangled dreams that softly sway.
In every heart, where magic stays,
Shadows dance in scarlet haze.

Flames Whisper Through Glistening Veils

Flames whisper through glistening veils,
In the night, where magic trails.
Each flicker tells a story bright,
Of ancient dreams in quiet flight.

A dance of fire, a glow so sweet,
Where courage and destiny meet.
The warmth of hope ignites the soul,
As woven threads begin to roll.

Through veils of mist, the flames do twine,
In every flicker, a secret sign.
With every pulse, a chance to rise,
To kindle dreams beneath the skies.

In molten pools, reflections gleam,
Carrying whispers of a dream.
In shadows cast, our wishes spin,
Through glistening veils, the light pours in.

So gather close, let spirits soar,
With flames that dance forevermore.
In every heart, where boldness dwells,
Flames whisper through glistening veils.

Shimmering Echoes of Forgotten Ashes

In the hush of woods where shadows dwell,
Whispers of the past weave their silent spell.
A flicker of light on a cold, dark stone,
Dreams dance like fire, yet we stand alone.

Ghosts of the flame rise on midnight's breath,
Stories of laughter entwined with death.
Silhouettes waltz beneath the star's keen gaze,
Life's fragile moments trapped in a blaze.

Embers aglow in the heart of the night,
Resilience sparked from a lingering light.
Through veils of silence, forgotten we roam,
Seeking the embers that once were our home.

With each scattered ash, a promise once made,
A spark of existence that never can fade.
Held in a memory, soft as a sigh,
The echoes of laughter rise up to the sky.

When the Sun Bleeds Into the Night

As the day whispers, it spills forth its gold,
Crimson and amber, its stories unfold.
A canvas of hues in the twilight's embrace,
Secrets unfurl in the darkening space.

With shadows a-dancing, the chill starts to creep,
The sun, like a dreamer, drifts softly to sleep.
Shores of the sunset, with waves that collide,
Hearts find their rhythm in the turn of the tide.

When the sky bleeds into the night's velvet throng,
Every heartbeat echoes a lingering song.
The stars breathe in whispers, their glow gently tight,
Binding the edges of day into night.

As dusk claims the light with its cool, tender hand,
We gather the twilight like grains of soft sand.
In the space between moments, the world seems to hold,
Wonders that shimmer in colors untold.

Infusion of Heat in Chasing Hues

In the dawn of the waking, colors ignite,
Chasing the shadows that linger in flight.
Brushstrokes of passion, the canvassed sky,
Awakens the heart, sets the spirit to fly.

With every horizon, new shades take their form,
A fusion of brilliance, a dance in the storm.
Golds blend with blushes, in fervent embrace,
Colors bleed softly, a tender, warm trace.

From the echoes of twilight to midday's bright glare,
Life pours in layers with whispers of flair.
Each moment is painted, a stroke of delight,
A vivid infusion, alive in the light.

In hues that caress us, vibrant and bold,
Stories unravel, both tender and old.
With each stroke of fate, we chase after dreams,
Finding our courage in the limpid streams.

Light Fractured by the Crimson Tide

Under the moon's gaze, the waters conspire,
Rippling reflections, a dance of desire.
Crimson waves crash with a fierce, wild call,
Where echoes scatter, and shadows will fall.

Each wave tells a story, both tragic and sweet,
Of journeys uncharted, of hearts that compete.
In the rhythm of tides, the world seems to breathe,
Threads of emotion woven with ease.

The light splits asunder, revealing the deep,
Mysteries hidden in secrets they keep.
A fracture of beauty in nature's bold game,
We gather the pieces, embracing the flame.

When twilight descends on the shimmering shore,
Whispers of longing beckon evermore.
In the dance of the evening, life takes a ride,
In the light fractured softly by the crimson tide.

The Blush of Dawn's Restless Heart

In the hush of morning's light,
The blush of dawn begins to fight.
Whispers of a night long past,
In dreams we found, our love held fast.

Mountains bathe in golden hue,
The world awakes, fresh and new.
Pattering raindrops on the leaves,
Nature hums, as hope retrieves.

Chasing shadows, light's embrace,
In the dawn, we find our place.
Time slips by, a fleeting dance,
In every heart, a hopeful glance.

With each heartbeat, secrets shared,
In this moment, souls laid bare.
The blush of dawn, a restless spark,
Igniting dreams that once were dark.

And as the sun climbs ever high,
We spread our wings, prepared to fly.
A canvas painted bright and bold,
In every hue, a story told.

Ascension Amidst the Silken Gloam

In the gloam where shadows weave,
A tapestry woven by those who believe.
Softly, the whispers call my name,
Eager hearts, aflame with the same.

Crimson threads in twilight's grace,
Dancing light, a tender embrace.
Beyond the mist where dreams ascend,
Hope's gentle hand, a trusted friend.

Stars awaken, one by one,
Witnesses to the day begun.
In this quiet, a breath is drawn,
Life is reborn at each new dawn.

As shadows fade and visions bloom,
Every heart dispels the gloom.
The silken path leads ever near,
To find our strength, to conquer fear.

So let us rise in unity,
Together bound, in harmony.
Ascent to heights where love resides,
Amidst the gloam, our spirit guides.

Flickering Dreams in a Crimson Sea

In the depths of a crimson sea,
Flickering dreams call to me.
Riding waves on a silvery crest,
In this realm, we find our quest.

Moonlight dances on water's skin,
Echoes of laughter linger within.
On sails of hope, we drift afar,
Guided by each twinkling star.

Secrets lie within the tide,
Where hidden wonders dare to hide.
Upon each crest, the stories soar,
In every dream, forevermore.

Casting nets of starlit wishes,
Catching moments, fleeting kisses.
In this ocean, wild and free,
Love shall bloom eternally.

As dawn arrives on the horizon's edge,
We find our footing, make our pledge.
Together we'll sail, hand in hand,
In this crimson sea, we shall stand.

A Whisper of Flame at Twilight's Veil

As twilight drapes the world in gold,
A whisper of flame, a tale unfolds.
Fires flicker in the gathering dark,
Igniting dreams with a fervent spark.

Beneath the canopy of dusky skies,
Where the last of daylight softly sighs.
In this moment, hearts entwine,
A secret bond, forever divine.

Glimmers of hope in the gentle night,
Painting shadows with sheer delight.
Each ember tells a story bright,
A dance of souls in the soft moonlight.

As stars awaken, they beckon near,
With every flicker, we conquer fear.
A whisper of flame, a guiding light,
Sustaining us through the long night.

In the silence, our spirits soar,
Creating magic forevermore.
At twilight's veil, we find our fate,
A whisper of love that won't abate.

www.ingramcontent.com/pod-product-compliance
Ingram Content Group UK Ltd.
Pitfield, Milton Keynes, MK11 3LW, UK
UKHW021629200125
4187UKWH00003B/69

9 781805 635055